ULIAQ's Amazing Animals: Snowy Owl

WRITTEN BY
Amelia Spedaliere

ILLUSTRATED BY
Amanda Sandland

Hi! My name is Uliaq, and I love animals. One of my favourite animals is the snowy owl.

Snowy owls are amazing!

1.5 m

64 cm

70 cm

4

Snowy owls are big birds.

Females are bigger than males. Males have a body length of up to 64 centimetres, and females have a body length of up to 70 centimetres.

Snowy owls have a wingspan of up to 1.5 metres. That's really big!

Male snowy owls can be completely white or have a few dark speckles. Female snowy owls have dark speckles all over their feathers.

Snowy owls' feathers help them **camouflage** on the snowy tundra.

male

female

7

Snowy owls are birds of **prey**, which means they hunt their food. They hunt small animals like lemmings. Lemmings are their favourite meal.

Snowy owls have big, sharp **talons** to catch their prey.

Yikes, those are sharp!

Let's look at the map!

Most snowy owls stay in the Arctic all winter long, but some fly south.

Snowy owls live alone or in pairs.

12

Snowy owls build their nests on raised ground.

Baby snowy owls are called chicks. Chicks are born around May. The female snowy owl sits on the eggs while the male brings her food and protects the area.

Snowy owls can hunt both during the day and at night.

Snowy owls have great hearing and amazing eyesight. Their big yellow eyes can see lemmings a long way off.

Once snowy owls spot their prey, they fly silently toward it. They use their big, powerful wings to get close.

Look at those wings! Cool!

When they swoop down, they can use their talons to catch their prey quickly.

I told you. Snowy owls are amazing!
That's why they are one of my
favourite animals.

What do you like about snowy owls?

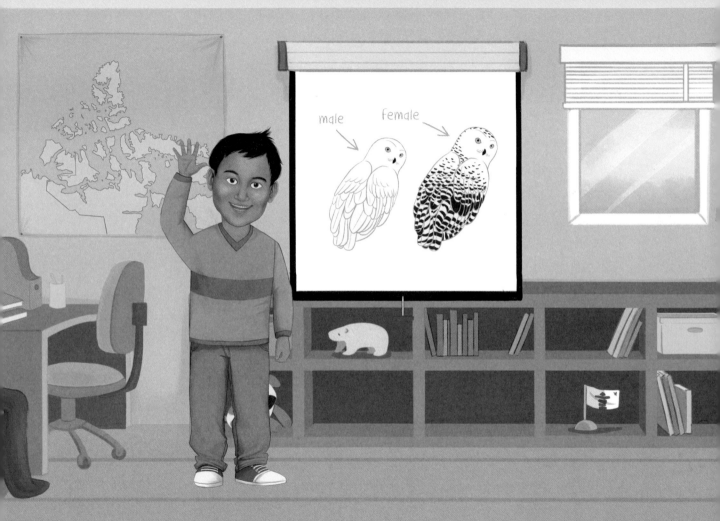

Glossary

camouflage
an animal's ability to blend in with its surroundings, making it hard to see.

prey
an animal that is hunted by another animal.

talons
the sharp claws of birds of prey.